LITERATURE & LANGUAGE DEPT.
CHICAGO PUBLIC LIBRARY
400 SOUTH STATE STREET
CHICAGO, IL 60605

3576
.A517
044
1998

HWLCLT

DEER TABLE LEGS

Chicago Public Library

T5-AOC-231

Deer table legs : poems.

DISCARD

JUN 1999

DEER TABLE LEGS

POEMS BY
Katayoon Zandvakili

THE UNIVERSITY OF GEORGIA PRESS
Athens and London

Published by the University of Georgia Press
Athens, Georgia 30602
© 1998 by Katayoon Zandvakili
All rights reserved
Designed by Kathi Dailey Morgan
Set in Electra
Printed and bound by Maple-Vail
The paper in this book meets the guidelines for
permanence and durability of the Committee on
Production Guidelines for Book Longevity of the
Council on Library Resources.

Printed in the United States of America
02 01 00 99 98 P 5 4 3 2 1

Library of Congress Cataloging in Publication Data
Zandvakili, Katayoon.
  Deer table legs : poems / by Katayoon Zandvakili.
    p. cm. — (Contemporary poetry series)
  ISBN 0-8203-2072-2 (pbk. : alk. paper)
  I. Title. II. Series : Contemporary poetry series
  (University of Georgia Press)
  PS3576.A517D44 1998
  811'.54—dc21   98-23350
                         CIP
British Library Cataloging in Publication Data available

to the two spirits in the mirror;

tremors—the good people in the house

ACKNOWLEDGMENTS

With deep gratitude to Brenda Hillman, Kate Johnson-Phillips, John High, Stephanie Strickland, and Bin Ramke. With love, for my parents and brother.

The poems "county," "love letter," and "The people in my country" appeared in *Massachusetts Review* 39, no. 2 (summer 1998).

CONTENTS

1. *The Lying Mango*

His eyes—this will be important later, perhaps   3
He says to look in his eye and I do   4
You took *rain* the wrong way   5
I think I helped you in your apartment that night   6
Bus stops in front of the window   7
Reading Sam Shepard plays   8
He comes into the room   10
because you ran with him at the beach   11
No Trespassing (Private Beach)   12
This is the hard part   13

2. *Body Light Houses*

Ophelia (The Prickly Pear), Drifting   17
I was wrong to trust the boy who wanted my tongue   18
You turn to me   19
Think of the gauzy face inside   20
county   21
love letter   22

3. *Three Horses in January*

Sound carries across water in winter, rowing   25
(my whole trouble)   26
They think I am one way   27
When we were talking   28
We sample paint labels together   30
The people in my country   31

4. Ponce de Leon

like what Lucy said about tigers lying in tall, tall grass   35
(Dog paces the room like yesterday's bone: zoo, zero)   36
I had just lost the blue dime child   37
He got married   38
walking in hallways long and clinical   39
Jerkfish   40

5. The Green Troubadour

deer table legs   45
In the fall, she finds a sister in a man   48
Either/Or, 1.   49
Either/Or, 2.   50
Either/Or, 3.   51
Four forgotten dreams: cloudy arms. Violets finagle in our time.   52
"I tried that already, I had passion. For two years. It didn't work."   53
Fortuna: Doves' Eggs   54
When I saw his forearm   56
I Called You So You Would Tell Me It Would Be Different   57
Marcus and his felt hat   58
the green troubadour returned in chains to answer for the
    Pied Piper   59
I felt your thigh across the distance of the city   60
When We Were   61
and the pink table   63

6. Fish Graces

These Fish Beauties, 1.   67
These Fish Beauties, 2.   68
These Fish Beauties, 3.   69
These Fish Beauties, 4.   70
You and me: the picture of the buffalo at the canyon   72
The Boy in the White Shirt, a parody   73
She says: We'd make good famous people   74

Fandango—tripping across (light)   75
the Boy & the Girl   76
In an open jalopy at night   77
One garbage man gives a rose to another   78
Remember going up to Lake George in the winter and having his tape
    to listen to?   79

DEER TABLE LEGS

1. THE LYING MANGO

His eyes—this will be important later, perhaps—are green-grey swirls:
not blue, not hazel.

The rear view mirror casts a rectangle
mask onto his face so from the side his eyes
look like violets.

Before, he laughed because he was happy.

She wants to fall in with him like the round and round of the attic.
The cruelties, a shrine of jewels on a dry riverbed, stop her. She has to
trust the water, that it will pick up again.

The sizzling grey of that highway going into Monterey, 156, like a line
of eye.

He says to look in his eye and I do, and there I find a snake and wolf, grey-green: a blue triangle.
It's not solace.

The sky—you can hardly look
at it but you do anyway.

A real wolf with long dark hair.

John, am I beginning now? If I were a brick
in a Viennese
wall, maybe I'd be happy.

He is walking away on Union Street. Actually, he is walking the same way I am, getting smaller and bigger, in and out around the trees, in a white prairie shirt. He is far away, distinct: Napoleon waving good-bye in the afternoon airport—

"I'm not impressed," he said, "with your friend's problems, the fact that you've never had sex"—

You took *rain* the wrong way, took it to mean something removed, rehearsed, once-seen about you. But I am with you satisfied as a tortoise shell.

> Those kids we passed
> in front of the store,
> there for another
> single purpose: faces
> unrecognizable.

White oleander thrown out to the wind, our faces so together we were away—

I think I helped you in your apartment that night. I needed to help and didn't know it.

The dog was not living with me, and instead of the spiders he would invite in, Feverfew floated on its belly and the blowfish belched. Water was nothing: after all, I dreamt water and sharks nightly.

I knew my pens like generals know their soldiers.
Your hand I could not bring myself to kiss.
Your face demanding at angles,
in other light—needy.

He is not desperate but there is a small orange square in him that's been ignited, it's alight; a small desperate square.

Bus stops in front of the window and I see her and me and her man and Marcus and the people in line all of a sudden with clear, outlined faces.

He'd knelt at my hospital bed saying, I think about you so much that if I told you, you'd say, You're just saying that because I'm dying. And I laughed. In a breakfast of ham and eggs, the hen is involved and the pig committed. We'll get married, you said. We'll make everything.   (Then changing lanes and angels were common.)

Friday afternoon rain and coffee in a dark wood corner. I want to talk to her and don't. Those driving, lousy questions; and this cheap, resourceful kaleidoscope tool like new water. We were all alive at the same time, around each other.

Reading Sam Shepard plays
in diners all over Tahoe—

And he says, "Don't look at me like you're watching a movie.
I'm not a movie. I'm really alone."

How long did you wait for him?   What was his name?   (Twice.)

Glenn Gould as an older man ["Motel Wawa"] standing next to the
ocean from behind the window, connected on the telephone and
saying it makes more sense to believe in the hereafter than in
oblivion. Did it end on "demise"? We all have the same death.

I was trying to explain that dull light, the looking away he gets in his
eyes, and I—we—said Disappearing, and he said Yes, I know about
that and did it some more.

His sarcasm bothered her. Then again sometimes she bothered
herself, so she could let it go. He didn't believe in God, and she said,
"How can my body be next to yours in the night and you not feel
God." But it's an ideal first, remembering a coin you've never seen:
a frog and a turtle, paddling to the creme moon.

She says, He does believe in God.
That he thanked me for being radiant by the window.
Thank you, he said.

She in her poverty and big-bellied
wistfulness is the motel room 200
miles away.

Exhaustion and love. He speaks
so coldly of our situation sometimes,

almost insults me. Holds silent like snow on the mountain top, and I
live all around. Then he comes looking for me in the red- and black-
mouthed cave. Every other man has intention, I say. We just believe
in longing, the coast.

———

Your plum shirt, rabid beginnings:
all mouth.
      Fine.

Cordoba is.

Waking with animals and sun in mind
to myself
      like a gradual 4-year-old, hair and fingers

This morning, on your kind side, having thought it all out in water,
swimming straight away.

He comes into the room and I keep thinking how I have a definite part of him inside me: giraffes crane their necks and then our shadow-yak-tree picture. Miso soup and white rice acquired after a stroll to the alley. In a raincoat, lifted, I am glowing like a caterpillar. The $600 brake job be damned, I'm pregnant. He's drawing Heliozx on the board, pillars and coliseums, says there is no center aisle

                 (the light in our Mouths—)

that was the basis of humanism.

because you're praying,
         he says,
and you don't know
what you're praying to

            light in our mouths

calling a fig a fig and a spade a shovel—we are en masse: well-read, heeding the glory

I say humanism is not a good thing and he laughs

because you ran with him at the beach
because you said haven't you had enough floor

your hair and heart a troubadour's
(hybrid gel)

in the kitchen three years before
crying about your married love—

dreaming the same dream as my dog

Mahler sprang us into forests
and then we were at the beach
with nowhere to go.
The lights to the left
made a casino circus
and the campers to the right were the mouth
of the cave—
                think about it: No resolve.

She scooped out the ice
cream as the dog licked
the floor. Tempted, you say.

No Trespassing (Private Beach)

Today:
                  the Valley
in front of the ocean—

          (your back)

A man/watching
his fields/water:
a yellow hat.

Finnish lips.
Eagle candy.

This is the hard part: knowing I wanted you to ask me to marry you—

2. BODY LIGHT HOUSES

Ophelia (The Prickly Pear), Drifting
— for Mary

Today, I did not/one
        unkind thing.
My pen lay in my pocket
        slimmer than usual.

In the gas station,
        I guessed at your witchcraft.
The credit card fit/the slot
        admirably. Red point.

A huge red ring, an
        agate, in the storefront
        window. We both know
        we won't buy it (we're
        late to a movie
        and I'm shy);
                we remember this
                each time we pass the store
                months later, when we're friends,
                when you do love me enough

    She has seriously. . . .

            It saves me for moments—
                God loving me as a serious adventure

            grace of
                grace thereby

I was wrong to trust the boy who wanted my tongue. Fell out of love with him the night before like a bronze coin plopping into the fountain. We speak three languages between us. There are acacias around the garage door and a line of wisteria out back. In the nobility of water, I find asphalt and sky, birds.

And you said—you said—stones and figs
and hullabaloo, rave starking moon and alehouse
quail, dandelion wine and airplanes, too—

Water washed you.
Polished stone and wheat.
Here you developed a face like a boy's, walked your dog on the beach wearing beads.

You turn to me
at jokes in a movie,
when you've never
done that.

I stand in my room later
and say out loud,
Please call
so I can feel kind.

———

You couldn't marry me because you didn't want to throw things away,
give and give—

everybody falls out of my heart
until the next man becomes first
love and I am a virgin again—

my hair, black currant tea today

long, wild walks:
(the level of) your fright in one fist
and your thirst

19

Think of the gauzy face inside. He turns. Go to Taos, my body says in the morning. Go to Taos and write your way out of this old, tired life into the right river, snow timbre: this is your task. Lift yourself. The desert is your family, cactuses: spirals and spokes. Don't wear heels. Driving into oblivion, you will have your own face—

Then we bought our parents long boxes of chocolates. Grandpa Joe told Charlie before he visited the Chocolate Factory, "You'll get it because you want it more."

county

Finding the stars over and over again
Nothing succeeds

You throw stones into the bed

A year later, she got married—

I could talk to you, and you
wanted to leave

"Wildly in love," you say, you
always stay, and I look out
from the porch at the mountain rising

Brandy the hot water under
the stars your neck. That I am toothless
in this sentence

The coast raves,
is the coast, an old ocean gazing:
the young man next day a boxer

You were granted three wishes
and used only two.
I was wasted

A kiss in the middle
of the highway: the spine of a road.
Five lights in the ocean

love letter

once haunted,
my face will take form

    ruins and a few fiend birds glued onto

    this fish's eye: iris

this girl's voice again

to stare at exotic cloth and when
we are horrible, to be very horrible together

intricate furniture of heart space

    (days forged from goodness)

3. THREE HORSES IN JANUARY

Sound carries across water in winter, rowing

The girl thinks about the child's voice,
a boy-girl voice/
I have to give my life to someone,
perhaps I will adopt.

If I had lived a violent life,
I would think, who
can slit my throat now?
I would think only
of the blade, of
things he would do
to my body.

      And the mosaics—
      the one with the 26 pieces
      of birds and flowers,
      pink and yellow

                    (my whole trouble)
               Foreignness of tongue
                        flashes
                a body's child of twelve
            cool and blue and iris, tall tree

The old mud tree: Kookaburra.
(Sat.)
Aim: New faces.

(Whole) summer on my left: dipped my arm in it some evenings—
teenagerhood and summer, whole summer—when the air was the
same as my skin

They think I am one way,
and actually I am of the Maderas
nut family. Clan. Group.

Feather
on her side, a fat grey
dead horse.
At the end
of the paddocks
in a puddle of hay.
We laughed
in black boots.

The man's profile chiseled into tile here,
he is the one.
(I was a French comedienne
all the while.)
We made money on stocks and bonds.

Ollie, Ollie, where are you today?
You came out to play, thanks.
Now, can you write your name without hate?

You in the tunnel.
Green (trees) and grey (fog) form a light.

When we were talking and I was trying to keep the peace about the
other—even with that, I was on the white inside of an egg room; blue
cotton candy, wavering: a hanging balance

They keep me as
a sugar white canary.
I can imagine other fathers
who would love me in navy-
black sweaters and glasses,
who would love jazz.
Mothers who walk
through the garden, salamander-
green and purple at midnight,
trailing the white of children
who have come undone.

―――

In the movie theater,
you feel the old cool and seventeen,
the black of sitting in a red
plush seat. Why are cinema
seats not mint green?

―――

He greeted the dog so warmly
above the green red hills

I looked out the window
for my brother, where was he?
I needed to go places just then. And

it takes me
another six years—no,
seven—to say

my father
my father
my father

We sample paint labels together, and she is the color of the trees in her shoulders this day. We read the names out loud and arrive as trees do. Thursdays I write about men and women (well, boys & girls really), but cities and robes, standing before columns at Persepolis, crying because you can't believe you're from here. This here.
You once stood over there—
You always wanted to leave.

The people in my country
sit beneath veils.
Their flesh giggles
and they assume.
What century is this? you ask,
kick-turn
in the pool.
Lines of humor,

the baroque clay
of their faces
absolves them
 —which is what you,
 on this side, want—
  absolution, all.

In the dog-
eat-dog, eat-
his-own-tail lettering
called grief,
 I am afraid they will love me
 more:
 take me into their faces
 and cloaks,
 make time-lapse photos of my missing hate.

(A browner thing than wool,
a river deadly with tree knots.)
So you keep company
with the gasoline cans
in the garage,
listen to strange music.

4. PONCE DE LEON

like what Lucy said about tigers lying in tall, tall grass—she found him and hurt him in a rage. Nothing was the same after. The blearing of notebooks clutched to the chest. Then was she mad and tender—and I only realized this the other day, lulling on the train—it made me wish I had the perfect sentence, an understanding like true body: those months of heaviness, the core of stopping. When the hills did such good.

———

Walls ran inside of you, rivers. Black hair meant nothing. One day, I thought I saw you on the pavement in Oakland. On the one hand, I was too good for you—or you were beneath me sort of because you had nothing to offer; on the other, it was really you who had left me. Who was the good person and who was the bad?

———

Past bones in the mirror, see the paper reflected inside. You sit clean as pie on a dark station bench, your sins visited upon the dog lying ragamuffin—the air wears heavy with the scent of memories. Remember this   and this? The dog's coat blows like a wheat field. Romeo and Juliet so pure they left their lives.

(Dog paces the room like yesterday's bone: zoo, zero)

What fills the crevice my neck forms as I lean into the bathroom sink? Fundamental reckoning. Because I got here. This wasn't always me. And so: voice.

When you touch the cold spot with air, you make a kitten sound, says the voice teacher.
What is this? When I breathe, I am still holding on to my stomach, which I don't understand what — it looks like.

On the other hand, not what makes her slump in her chair but what would make her sit up?
Got a glimpse of the two women walking about.

The hitch in the breath.
It's okay if they hear your voice, see your face and body.

I wanted to make animal sounds and didn't. The eyes worked too hard. Poor eyes.
The possibility of elbows: light.

I had just lost the blue dime child. We were in a room with menacing types, some on drugs, some just harsh. We were taking a test. I stood and paced. Then I sat by the plants opposite the door to get help with the chlorophyll questions. Lambchop was a beautiful deer, not just a deer head—skinned, only hay inside for paranoia to translate into. The examination clock watched from the glowing pantry.

(I used to talk like that, I understood my mouth, tender linkages, and sweet melts. Breathing is easy, the teacher said. Make your skin disappear.)

There he was, the deer, his blue-grey liquid eyes on someone else's head, when he was from a green place entirely. It was like war.

He got married
On a hillside overlooking the sea
We fell to the floor in the car
Truffles
The grey house. Maples
The world dug out

        Tierra del Fuego,
        the jewel you fell from

walking in hallways long and clinical, maples touching the windows during windy spells

now an old woman laughs behind me in a nearly dark theater

Rabbit-like, I strove to get away.

Meanwhile, slipcovers and wolf hairs, green Studebakers line the drive, shaking rose loves and what else could happen to invade the upstairs—

Jerkfish

Running over stone and leaf
to stop stomach to stomach.
My self in a catbird cage
on high; it would never find
the moon. You had the strength
of rain in your voice—that
silver—later, you took this

     the wrong way. I only met you
once in my life, he wrote.
Your face came into mine
with the brilliance of teeth, loud water promises.

The stars as bright as polar
bears: shreds. All
mouth in their dignity and small
innocence—white (raucous
white) and infectious. The stars as proof
of what was chasing me then

and before
    (a child of nine,
      she ate the plaster from the walls):

proof of what
is chasing me now: the red dog
          eats/his own tail,/
        (I've become)

The stars as big as thumbs,
racing hybrids
curious as bears: like fingers,
gullible. Traveling alone in white space.
      Blue hills for eyes.

When I found my way
it was with you as bears: beyond (white).
And I understood form
though I was moving away from it,
and wanted dark

      though I was nearest
you. Entanglement forms
the newest bramble: ashamed

that I had never had a friend,
and now we were standing
on the side of the road.

If I tell you this,
all will be turned. We will move on.

One day in New York, I wrote:
      He is still big in his bones.
      I smile and move room to room.
      Ocean slabs against rock in Monterey.
      I am in my jeans like water.
      I have the feeling.

Hawk, telephone pole

Tahoe, turning a corner in snow
(the carriage dream
handkerchief
white gathering)

He was missing from my dreams
and I was, too. You held me
for three minutes on the side of the road.

5. THE GREEN TROUBADOUR

deer table legs

This is where you live with no further patience for Chess: the etiquette of fan and smile, sloping back.

The men I met fell from the tops of sentences. They promised hot-air balloon rides, would've stolen sheep. On the way up the mountain, they held silent. (Silence is power, the book said.) And in the winter of my young year, when I was desperate as wind, they laughed. It cannot be, I thought (am thinking it still) — but I talked to them, one by one, and they laughed.   In the same way perhaps that they didn't know about what had gone on before — like the rupture, burst — didn't know about the guide; it happened often enough. So I granted them interviews; they came to my photo shoots.

―――

We enter houses in fields ringing with thistles and impatiens (home, moody). Death comes later, in public: the smatter of white pavement, classic boots. Long arms in dark jackets. Monday follows Thursday. You leave the elevator and kiss me hard for good measure: step away like a faint red leaf—
Night carves out toy bridges.

―――

I saw her leave the book, saw the sun on the tabletop, knife on the bread. "Bagel" became "bread." I was writing for all time.

I am going to hold your baby. A sunny, clear picture. I want to understand the different waves of his head and body, the smiling eyes, the other riding out of me.

―――

he says he has never seen the ocean
and looks around the room nervously as Christopher Robin would
climbs out of the car and says he'll be right back
he pours coffee in a thermos and I watch like mermaids breathing
a leg of weight draped over me (: in the attic, a paperboy hat)
he calls people to say he's made love—oh no, they groan in
Chicago—when all he has done is kiss my hand like a stolen statue,
dropping to his knees as at deepest wood
the round of his white shoulders
at twilight we were on the bleachers by the river
      he was learning to run

———

But what of macadamia nuts/salt/a television producer/public battles in South/Carolina and baths
This man and woman/kissing/at our shared table are/not married. She is/plain and he is/rich. They/kiss again.
The woman/at the other table has/on the same exercise/socks I have in a drawer at home./
He leaves. I am working, I really am. His pants sag.
The rest of the day is accustomed exhilaration: spins.

———

You give me your money because you love me. We enter each other at night. Sometimes, we don't want to but we do anyway.
We could've left it for another time. Hands trail.

———

You scoffed at Grace Cathedral, the lamp overhead. Felt your teeth grow, the fine hair.

I was 27 and you were 28. We touched (afternoon teapots, deer table legs) in profile, startled by the word "we."

I wanted to make a film about cab drivers in other cities—not really, I wanted to want to.

In Europe, they wear wedding rings on the other hand.

The men I met, each one, an unspoken name living in a house on a beach. I made blue glass-cathedral slivers in a cone of tangerine night. No man could take that sort of life away, and no woman. Dog noses, like moose, were okay.

In the fall, she finds a sister in a man. She goes to him wanting to be swung onto his shoulders. You are like all the other men because you are about her. It grows green, greener. You hold your life then hers. Hold your heart and tumble down the hill. Selah.

Either/Or, I.

To carry that lime
habit, shot-in-the-arm, green-
blue-white
skin light

of the tub.
Your face

like someone else's entirely: circus
clown or a runaway's. Kiss

on top
of
the ferris wheel.
Follow him into the cave

when he is drunk
and broken, apish,
and nobody else will.

Bicycle across the ocean.
Four elements.
The road trip.

Aghast at a friend's moving into a different position.
He said, I called you eight times today.
Can you take care of yourself?
You've lost so much weight.

Either/Or, 2.

      When they lost him,

they were afraid this
would never happen again:
coming out of night restaurants
and leaning against a black gate to talk
      about old horse fools.

"You were running scared, and we were in love," she would later say.
They watched a lot of movies, good movies.

She said, I think
      I can say this, it has been long enough—
      and the old brown
      bear laughing in the background, singed.

Then she was open   and far
because she was/angry:
the people   before: (from
      whom)
And she stayed away   awhile,
      grazing—

Either/Or, 3.

You never anticipated the four/elements in the dog's response,
rose to shake his paw

The fish chased the lion through
                             snow landscape under the moon
the word "under"
                             he wanted to marry me like that, now I know

Four forgotten dreams: cloudy arms. Violets finagle in our time.

When he spoke, she went far away.
She once listened to a message three times
just to get its content. It was her own voice
he had left her.

Finding the malicious heart of the apple—Godfrey
frays, God fries—
mellifluous, he said, when
it sounded like a word I already knew and let go—
a corral word, pasture of cows.

"I tried that already, I had passion. For two years. It didn't work." The Napoleon/Brando mix and my death in small increments: over bridges.

I go out to a Japanese restaurant with him. The original him. He wants me to sit next to him; there I sit on a blue and white mat, bleached bench. When he holds my hand, I think of the boy whose happiness will be marred for a few days because I think I am leaving to fit a life rightly.   I never know how to touch him although I am a woman. Something has to be gotten out of the way first as a fact. His face is beautiful, the profile. We talk about highways and diners, churches in Europe. He'd said something once about a beautiful church in Pennsylvania, a tiny church.

Fortuna: Doves' Eggs

> I spend my life sitting, like an angel in a barber's chair
> —Arthur Rimbaud

The new suitor
names trees for me.
Stands tall and attentive
in a black coat. His back
is all we will remember of him.
We have what I call "the new trees."

The old love who is new
asks the wan, poking
thing under the light.
Borrows Neruda to say
you are purer than dreams.

And my folks,
orange peels drifting
out to sea,

make
me
pull
myself
up
by
the
hair.

The angels
arrive
and help,
tugging,
to show
rocks and water.

The beach fire mounts like a yell
with a red/brown drop.
Doves' eggs into foam.

The dogs save the cuffed man: scared, sacred.
I go to Taos, get my fortune told.

When I saw his forearm
on the table in the preview months later,
I thought: I wrote to that guy. I could see/myself with that guy once.

Balloons on a platform station,
7 o'clock red.

I Called You So You Would Tell Me It Would Be Different

Today I painted my life on the old bedmattress (animals and heat, colors, cows in color) and felt dim at night in the movie theater amidst the wash of other arms and lips, warm hats. I hated you and missed you, was worried over you. There was a sad new everyday feeling and I was holding a red feather behind my back, knowing I was going away from you, not knowing what would become of you; in the end, in that line of night and fishing lines, turning over in sleep and—your tale, your fish tale. Outside the church on the white steps, what did we say again?

So I call you when I'm not supposed to, want your voice to say, *good* and *always* and *you*, all the things that I don't have in me but talk, keep on talking, remind me

                    The tangy zebra, the sunny day inside the greenhouse, actors walking around the pool in turn-of-the-century fur, a photographer on her knees to an iris.

The dogs are howling. It is not a pretty thing.
When I thought of going home, it was like
the calm after dying. A tribute
to some swan. (You touch your hand
to the wall, and the country springs like a face.)

                    That I could not marry you, my kite love.
Although the field we crossed together. Although walking with you felt like a tree being split in half.

Marcus and his felt hat come and sit with me. He says all about calcium dioxide in bones and why water is beautiful to us. He brings up the lime habit and shoots his arm like a pro. I think all the time of the ocean at night, when we kissed the spine of the road and ran at the first sight of headlights. You say these lines. The white wash of the boulders; those crags. (I walk in the woods in the afternoon, breathing and thinking: Sometimes he maddens me.)

the green troubadour returned in chains to answer for the Pied Piper

he sees me rudely crossed over the line into male bodies: salamander.
he is in a beige raincoat, catching droplets
on the grass patch, says I'm thinking too much.

> He's smart—he's smart and he's hungry, really hungry. He
> knows about the compass in his hand, the grandfather clock,
> eternal stopwatch.

White armchairs in the foothills.
Three French tourists look my way.
In the bar, a journalist asks if he has written any poems lately.

His newfound arm on the back of my seat as I drive; rough cranberry
sweater. I turn to watch a building/when I needn't.
In an irksome triangle, the new suitor names trees for me; jaw drops;
parade of boats—

I'm standing against the heater, putting clothes on.
Ready to lose the one man I have been able to talk to.

I felt your thigh across the distance of the city.
There was a scream then a red bus.
We penciled in your name and flowers, the grave.
Ate gigot, rack of lamb —

Palms on grand foreheads of beach.
The triangle of the ocean today;
green-eyed white gathering

A cheeseburger above the rose
cliff. He takes you along
another path, then runs

        at white-pine freedom:

                Pilot —

When We Were

She drove me there
to let me see. She
wanted this.

The man at the foot of the wheelchair in the sand said,
"In all the cities of the world," in French.

The sand, cold, reassuring mesh;
you don't know, but the weight of you,
it goes back into the earth.
We walk away lifted.

We walk away from the people staying
to watch the sun more.
Walk up the street
into dogs and jasmine: a borrowed collective

>Getting out of the car in New York,
>you say, "I feel like the horizon"—
>and the air like our skin

So thankful this afternoon, photographing
rock and water in Monterey.
The red cliffs with their sheer noses, dresses

>—because the air is like our skin—
>no different—and I couldn't imagine
>having hurt you

The black horse and the white horse
on the hill. "The two of them
haven't moved," you say, moving your salad.

From the wood table of their anniversary, the strangers watched us.
We didn't watch the horizon, like we thought.
We talked about the papers in front of us: they glowed.

Water moving over rock.
You never knew this. The sky's face,
doubly bald.

To think that we were so thankful,
when we were.

And then, just as we — just as — I mean
— we stopped. We just stopped.

And the next day, the next day —

and the pink table
of fruit in grass
high as cranes
what lack did I have

you say I have something
inside that you promised me
I didn't and now you will take
it back

the sky is shark blue
green perfect-high-school-morning
        eyes: mango

                the tenement buildings the fierce multiplex windows

6. FISH GRACES

These Fish Beauties, 1.

you and me and friends like fish   keeping watch, horrid
          either understanding
                              or baking in an unkempt sun of absence

Why were we given this (love)?
How/to keep it? Don't we—dare

When you spoke/
such roundedness—
empty, filled-in—I watched you—
you pronounced—so
beautifully—I kept
"you"

                god-food: prunes, figs/on high,
                          persimmons like hands

These Fish Beauties, 2.

you and me and a strange woman's hair
                       between us

with McTeague's gold tooth
                       on the beach

and the childhood gate
every time you went
                       away and I was left
                       with that special feeling of dying

      and then your back turned:
                     gaze
you and me and the stars
                   in the buildings: a fortnight
                   bold and beguiling

petting the turtle's head for elegance
finding home
finding fish
finding the other leg
     your paw
        shrimp perhaps stare blind
        finding fins and lies, fingers

the horse mystery
               elegiac
monastery
      I mean, (convent) run to—

These Fish Beauties, 3.

that you are the color of the trees
                        in your shoulders this day

he said, come here. Stand by the lamp shade — look out at the snow.
          At 2 a.m. partings there is no good end

I told myself I would go back and find the old woman —
which was a false goal because then I did find her,
and she said, "You smell like your childhood."

She got out of the car like before:
pink plastic basket in hand, chador in her mouth.
She prays me daily, says I am forgetting
her again.

No lilac hills or trumpet tunes.
Her skirt was nice, my life
rounded out at month's end, and she
who raised me got out of the car.

          I saw how the other girl
          watched, I saw —
          how —

All the faces of the unbelieving stone.
Coming away from the streets and the dogs and the women in black.

These Fish Beauties, 4.

you and me and the whole pot of mango
                                        tea café
we never went to cafés before: and now, expectation

you and me and the two women talking psychology
on the hill, Moses and Abraham, the lambs

our big fears like hatchets

standing around later:
a case of unmemory —
trying to conjure up the heat

you and me and his one red ear

paring down our lives to a walk on the beach

        You cut to the quick of a person.
        I ran a sword along the belly
        of a map of the world — a hat:
        the laughter of 2 women — one old,
                the other younger

        The houses there
        folded in streets
        with ballet arms for trees —
        You bought me *L'Amour*, Stendhal,
        and forgot to give it to me.

       I thought horses were the belly of the world;
       they weren't. The hills, in
            fear and laughter

You and me like two engineers talking at a table

               I went to Deauville once. Twice. Took
               the train and stood thinking of racehorses
               and mandarins out the window.

                       The paint was a good horse. He stood 6 hands
                                        high, practically.

You and me: the picture of the buffalo at the canyon—
              a hundred thousand cathedrals with their heads
                  turned downward,
              he wrote. Your picture was more frozen across—
              more weed and pond. I could see them chewing. Then
              you, your two guy friends who were straight
              with you, the car loops in the night.

You and me: trying to figure out the oil
              in the air. We try to choose
              words instead of being picked by them.

You and me and the coldness we use because we love each other so much and know of no other way.

You and me and 45,000 pounds
              and $100,000 dollars. U.S.
              Bah, what do I know of money?
You and me: the freelance romantics.
              I'll sell my stock.

You and me and the Boy in the White Shirt.
              Was I with you when you asked him?
              Didn't he ask you why you didn't do it there?
              Talk to the person you're supposed to talk to.

The Boy in the White Shirt, a parody.
He believed and played
an invisible guitar.

>   —Why were you so dead my love It's
>   the question of your life. In the other version
>   of mine, every street seems crowned in regality,
>   procession. Like fruit, it yields. Where I offer
>   people things, I am let go.

People have good conversations. They speak of cameras and souls.
"The screen."
They argue whether Eleanor was beautiful when/she was young, and
Lucy says yes, she was.

>   Finally, they stop talking   for the benefit of passersby.

She says: We'd make good famous people.
                        We'd make good dead people, too.

you and me and fruit markets
one big screenplay
boulevards in avalanche

Saw Audrey Hepburn marry a billionaire in a b&w movie. She ran along a train platform and she was Audrey Hepburn.

you and me

You and me and the other graciousness,
other marriage

                a marriage
      like minions'. Centaurs.
      Marriage as separate noun, geometric
      light—amorphous.

They played "Fascination" in their hotel room.

Nice to have money to go to a café in the morning, be sparse with—

Fandango—tripping across (light)—

varicose veins

Our differences in finding a house. It was difficult
somehow—we couldn't walk into a space natural as flowers,
succumbing: an extension of breathing and eyes

Was it our jealousy?
I am in this room now. I won't be in minutes. Cancer is awful/You
only lost a baby—not even, a seed. Thank God./ I do think you were
in love with him more than he was in love with you—

> We wanted a house that was a body, a story:
> natural telling. Gross mountain.
> Do we have what we had?

This is his way of getting back at me
because he knows I don't love him.
Is this his way? Talk-talk.   He's
a handsome—wait, Cancer—boy.
How can you laugh through this?
How can you wear clothes like stone?
> I should like to wear clothes
> like the prairie. Gratuitous ending.

the Boy & the Girl

Sometimes you look at a boy and he looks at you from
across the street for the first time like you
share a secret, when you don't want to share anything.

>And there's the bridge of death (after
>sex:) silver-grey mostly and traversed by
>a white horse.

He makes you feel the wanting you have in common,
the have before had. He can't give you anything,
he says, has nothing to offer.   O how you lie,
>you think, seeing his hand, his shirt
>and feet—you, in lemon sheets.
>You are thin, he says.

His face, the second face you hold, you know
you are going to be looking at for a long time.
It's the kind of face that sits by the fireplace,
listens into the night, wears the sleeve of years.

>You are tired of playing
>games. So you state
>your intentions. I want
>to grow seahorses, you say.
>The males get pregnant.

The first boy, when he kissed you, he
kissed you with lots of saliva.
He said what it feels like to hold a trembling
woman in his arms.

In an open jalopy at night, I turn and see a sort of tail, this bay road we are traveling on, and then dolphins. I want to photograph them and hold the camera, no flash, to my eye. A red grey dot like dusty fame settles on the boy. He is in the water, and I take it without the moon because I remember the moon is in the upper-left corner and I am hoping it will turn out. He was in a blue/white shirt, cherry-bombing.   He had a fantastic life. He was a son.

One garbage man gives a rose to another.
We name possible children
in movie theaters before the curtain:
Hawthorn & Tulla, Narcy my
daughter

clouds like scrubbed eggs
       white and hardy
one like a pointed elephant's head carton

       (her forehead, her eyes)

                        The Fields of Athenry

      I throw an opal ring out of
      the car window, Irish fields—
      remember the harbour in Deauville

Remember going up to Lake George in the winter and having his tape to listen to? Remember kissing him? The shades, lavender, his hands everywhere and the fine evil force in the world next door. My face was in his hands.

THE CONTEMPORARY POETRY SERIES
Edited by Paul Zimmer

Dannie Abse, *One-Legged on Ice*
Susan Astor, *Dame*
Gerald Barrax, *An Audience of One*
Tony Connor, *New and Selected Poems*
Franz Douskey, *Rowing Across the Dark*
Lynn Emanuel, *Hotel Fiesta*
John Engels, *Vivaldi in Early Fall*
John Engels, *Weather-Fear: New and Selected Poems, 1958–1982*
Brendan Galvin, *Atlantic Flyway*
Brendan Galvin, *Winter Oysters*
Michael Heffernan, *The Cry of Oliver Hardy*
Michael Heffernan, *To the Wreakers of Havoc*
Conrad Hilberry, *The Moon Seen as a Slice of Pineapple*
X. J. Kennedy, *Cross Ties*
Caroline Knox, *The House Party*
Gary Margolis, *The Day We Still Stand Here*
Michael Pettit, *American Light*
Bin Ramke, *White Monkeys*
J. W. Rivers, *Proud and on My Feet*
Laurie Sheck, *Amaranth*
Myra Sklarew, *The Science of Goodbyes*
Marcia Southwick, *The Night Won't Save Anyone*
Mary Swander, *Succession*
Bruce Weigl, *The Monkey Wars*
Paul Zarzyski, *The Make-Up of Ice*

THE CONTEMPORARY POETRY SERIES
Edited by Bin Ramke

J. T. Barbarese, *New Science*
J. T. Barbarese, *Under the Blue Moon*
Stephanie Brown, *Allegory of the Supermarket*
Scott Cairns, *Figures for the Ghost*
Scott Cairns, *The Translation of Babel*
Richard Chess, *Tekiah*
Richard Cole, *The Glass Children*
Martha Collins, *A History of a Small Life on a Windy Planet*
Martin Corless-Smith, *Of Piscator*
Christopher Davis, *The Patriot*
Juan Delgado, *Green Web*
Wayne Dodd, *Echoes of the Unspoken*
Wayne Dodd, *Sometimes Music Rises*
Joseph Duemer, *Customs*
Candice Favilla, *Cups*
Casey Finch, *Harming Others*
Norman Finkelstein, *Restless Messengers*
Dennis Finnell, *Belovèd Beast*
Karen Fish, *The Cedar Canoe*
Albert Goldbarth, *Heaven and Earth: A Cosmology*
Pamela Gross, *Birds of the Night Sky/Stars of the Field*
Kathleen Halme, *Every Substance Clothed*
Jonathan Holden, *American Gothic*
Paul Hoover, *Viridian*
Austin Hummell, *The Fugitive Kind*
Claudia Keelan, *The Secularist*
Maurice Kilwein Guevara, *Postmortem*
Caroline Knox, *To Newfoundland*
Steve Kronen, *Empirical Evidence*
Patrick Lawler, *A Drowning Man Is Never Tall Enough*
Sydney Lea, *No Sign*
Jeanne Lebow, *The Outlaw James Copeland and the Champion-Belted Empress*
Phillis Levin, *Temples and Fields*

Gary Margolis, *Falling Awake*
Mark McMorris, *The Black Reeds*
Jacqueline Osherow, *Conversations with Survivors*
Jacqueline Osherow, *Looking for Angels in New York*
Tracy Philpot, *Incorrect Distances*
Donald Revell, *The Gaza of Winter*
Martha Ronk, *Desire in L.A.*
Martha Ronk, *Eyetrouble*
Aleda Shirley, *Chinese Architecture*
Pamela Stewart, *The Red Window*
Susan Stewart, *The Hive*
Terese Svoboda, *All Aberration*
Terese Svoboda, *Mere Mortals*
Lee Upton, *Approximate Darling*
Arthur Vogelsang, *Twentieth Century Women*
Sidney Wade, *Empty Sleeves*
Marjorie Welish, *Casting Sequences*
Susan Wheeler, *Bag 'o' Diamonds*
C. D. Wright, *String Light*
Katayoon Zandvakili, *Deer Table Legs*